# WHO FOUND AMERICA?

A GOLDEN GATE JUNIOR BOOK

Childrens Press, Chicago

# WHO FOUND AMERICA?

By Johanna Johnston

Pictures by Anne Siberell

**Library of Congress Cataloging in Publication Data**

Johnston, Johanna.
  Who found America?

    SUMMARY: Explains in simple terms the discovery
and settlement of America.
    "A Golden Gate junior book."
    1. America—Discovery and exploration—
Juvenile literature. [1. America—Discovery
and exploration] I. Siberell, Anne, illus.
II. Title.
E101.J74   973.1   73-8773
ISBN 0-516-08747-9

Picture, top page 28, Reprinted by permission of Ebony Magazine.

Long, long, long ago
there were no people at all in America—
only wild animals and birds.
And then, far off in the north of Asia,
where some people did live,
a few hunters and their families
began going farther and farther,
looking for game.
Until finally they were wandering across
an ice-covered sea
that separated Asia from America.

These hunters kept on wandering,
following the game,
but when they came at last
to warmer country
they decided to stay.

They were the very first people
to find America.
Today we call them Indians.
And for thousands of years
they were the only people in America.
They spread across the country.
They divided into tribes
and built villages.
But nobody else, anywhere in the world,
even knew America existed.

And then, far across the sea to the east,
in the northern part of Europe,
some men began to grow very brave
about sailing out on the ocean.
A few of them sailed farther and farther
and farther
until at last they came to a northern part
of America.

They were the Norsemen.
Their leader was Leif Ericson.
They were the first men
from across the Atlantic Ocean
to find America.

But the land seemed very wild to them.
The Indians were not friendly.
Soon they sailed back across the sea
to their homeland.
And by and by
they forgot all about the
new land they had found.

After a long, long time
some other men
in a southern land
also began to grow brave
about sailing far out to sea.
Some of them sailed farther
and farther
until they came to
a southern part of America.

They were Africans.
No one knows the name of their leader.
And they stayed in the part of
South America they had found.
They did not go home again.
And so people across the sea
still did not know
about America.

Another long, long time went by.

Then some more people grew braver
about sailing out on the sea.
There was one man who thought
that if he sailed far enough
he would come to India or China.
He set out with three ships and
sailed and sailed
until he came to some islands
which he thought must be near India.
Really, these islands were near America.

This man was Christopher Columbus
and he was Italian.
But some of the men with him
were Spanish.

And he had a pilot
whose name was Nino,
and he was an African.

All of them sailed around the islands.
They found Cuba and
they found Puerto Rico
and lots of other islands.

Then they sailed back home
and they told everybody about
the new lands they had found.

So now, for the first time,
people in Europe
knew there was land across the sea.
And more and more of them began coming.
Some men from England came
and sailed along the northern coast
of America.
And some men from Holland came.

A Spaniard named Ponce de León came
and he went on past the islands
that Columbus had found
and landed on North America itself,
where Florida is today.

Lots of other Spaniards came,
and some Africans too.
There was an African named Estevan
who was shipwrecked off Florida.
When he got to the land
*he walked*
all the way from Florida,
through Alabama and Mississippi and
Louisiana—and farther yet—
to Mexico.

After that, Estavan
took another trip,
up into the hills and deserts of
New Mexico,
where he met the Indians who
lived in pueblos.

Soon more and more and more people—
men and women and children too—
were coming from across the sea
and settling in America.
Spaniards came and built towns
in Florida and the far west.

Some men came from England and
settled in Virginia.
After awhile some Africans
were also landed there.
And they all began making farms.

Then those English men and women whom
we call Pilgrims came,
and they settled
on the coast of Massachusetts.

Some people came from Holland
and they settled farther south
and started the town we now call
New York.

Some men came from France
and they settled up in Canada
and along the great northern rivers.

Who found America?
All of them were finding America—
and there was still more of America
to discover.

The towns along the coasts grew bigger.
But there was still
much, much *more* land,
away from the coast—
land that only the Indians knew.

Now men began exploring
to discover that land.

There was a man named
Daniel Boone
who went farther and farther inland,
into the woods where the bears
and the Indians were,
until he found that part of the land
which is now Kentucky and Indiana.

There was a man from the West Indies,
named Jean DeSable,
who traveled up the Mississippi River
into the same sort of wild country—
and finally he started a trading post
that became Chicago.

And there were more and more and more people,
from every land across the sea,
finding America.
And all the while they were doing that,
something else was happening too.

They were all becoming Americans themselves.
Not Spaniards, not Englishmen,
not Dutchmen, not Frenchmen,
not Africans,
but Americans.

And so, when kings across the sea
tried to make laws for them as if
they still belonged in Europe,
the people suddenly realized
those laws did not fit them any more.
And they fought to be free.

The first man to fall
in the cause of liberty
was an American named Crispus Attucks.

All kinds of Americans
helped in the fight after that—
Paul Revere and Molly Pitcher,

Salem Poor, and quite a few Indians too.

And, of course,
George Washington.

And, finally, they were free
to be Americans.

Who had found America?
All of them.
And all kinds of people
have kept on finding America
ever since.

YOU find America,
one way or another,
every day.

*There were more and more people from every land across the sea finding America . . . and all the while they were doing that something else was happening—they were all becoming Americans themselves. Not Spaniards, not Englishmen, not Dutchmen, not Frenchmen, not Africans, but Americans . . . Who found America? All of them . . . and all kinds of people have kept on finding America ever since.*

In this unusual book author Johanna Johnston presents a unique view of American history, written especially for very young readers. Beginning with those ancient wanderers from northern Asia who crossed the Bering Sea to the North American continent so many thousands of years ago, she points up the significant milestones that led at long last to the founding of a new nation—always with emphasis upon the people, famous and obscure, who made America a reality. Artist Anne Siberell has illustrated the text with charming collages in full color, combining them with a number of historical engravings that add both flavor and authenticity to a delightful and meaningful book.

JOHANNA JOHNSTON'S interest in things American began in childhood when her family moved South each year to escape the rigors of winter in her native Chicago. Fascinated by the diversity of the country, she began early to delve into American history, a subject she has enthusiastically pursued ever since, as her many books for both children and adults on America's past will attest. *Thomas Jefferson, His Many Talents,* her first book of an historical nature for young people, won a Thomas Alva Edison Foundation award and was followed by *Together In America, A Special Bravery, Paul Cuffee, America's First Black Captain,* and *The Indians And The Strangers,* all published by Dodd, Mead. Miss Johnston is also the author of several distinguished adult biographies as well as a number of successful picture books for young children. She has lived for many years in New York City and spends summers in Arlington, Vermont.

ANNE SIBERELL is an award-winning graphic artist and a painter whose work has been exhibited throughout the United States. She has illustrated a number of children's books, including Mark Taylor's *Lamb, Said The Lion, I Am Here,* published by Golden Gate Junior Books in 1971, and *Passage To Drake's Bay* (William Morrow). She has also taught children's art classes. Mrs. Siberell is a native of Los Angeles and received her art training from UCLA and the Chouinard Art Institute. She now lives in Hillsborough near San Francisco with her husband and three sons.